AF359155

FROM EDEN

AITIJHYA MONDAL

Writer's Pocket

First published by Writer's Pocket in 2023

email: publish@writerspocket.com

Copyright © 2023 Aitijhya Mondal

cover design by Rutuja Shelke

All rights reserved.

ISBN-13: 978-93-6083-818-8

www.writerspocket.com

for baba and ma

to the ones who have lost

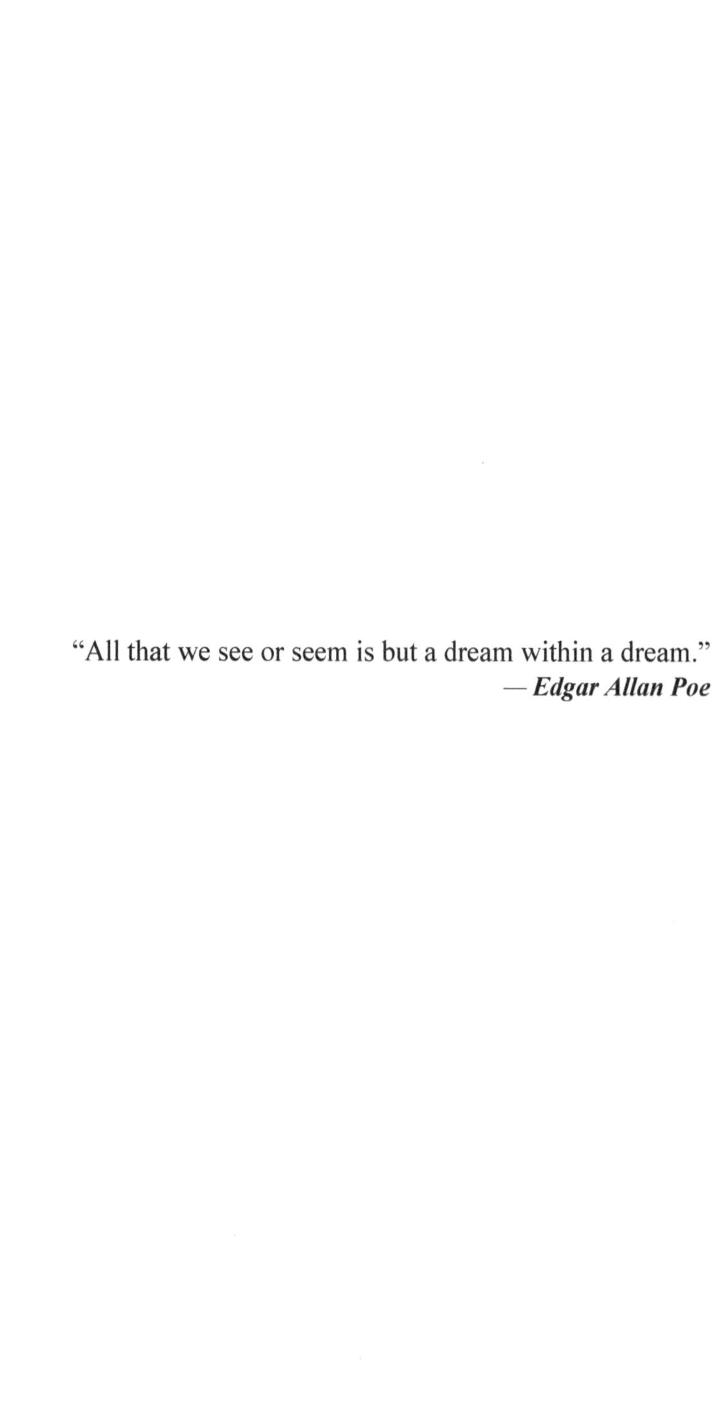

“All that we see or seem is but a dream within a dream.”
— *Edgar Allan Poe*

CONTENTS

ACKNOWLEDGMENTS

firstly, i would like to thank my parents without whom i probably would have stopped at the first page. thank you eqra for being my first reader, am forever indebted to you. special thanks to ruti for giving me strength and art, and for inspiring me every day with her strength. i apologise, to all my friends for asking the most agonizing questions known to man at the most gruesome times. i sincerely hope that this won't be my last time asking them. really grateful for my team at writer's pocket who made everything so accessible and easy. lastly to everyone around me, thank you. none of this would have been possible without you. you've inspired me to be who i am today. there is a little bit of each one of you in this book. i love you all.

Prologue

The **Garden of Eden** is the biblical paradise created by God, inhabited by the first humans- Adam and Eve. Though seemingly perfect and heavenly, the imperfect garden of Eden is what leads to the fall of humanity and loss of innocence. Adam and Eve must learn how to die first in order to live. Desirous of more than the paradise they already own, Adam and Eve fall from grace. And only when they fall from grace do they truly fall in love with each other. Thus lies the Garden of Eden, the rawest display of human vulnerability and desire.

Chapter One
winter
dies irae

and when life starts to fade away and insanity rolls in, will *you* be all that's left of me?

you love a very red, red liquid. you love wine. doubtless, i bring it to you. we will never be here again. we will freeze up and turn to stone, and our bodies will melt into this earth. if anything such as love had ever existed, it was pure in that bottle of red wine. it turned your cheeks to an adorable maroon. and when these days start to fade and insanity rolls in, will a bottle of wine be all that's left of us? and when you open your mouth, you devour whatever love's left of us; love crawls down your throat slowly and you're suddenly, so red. both of us are endlessly, in neverland. now every day that i wake up, fresh blood starts to feel like love sprouting up to my skin. i've never questioned you. love *is* what you told me love was. a very red, red liquid.

a red petal spoke to me in anguish. its anger spoke of you in unfamiliar tongues, i looked at it for hours on end, and it distorted into the colour of your eyes. somehow i remember them as a comfortable haven. but today as your eyes flicker in the dark, the only thing i witness is a vile blue rage. i lie by your side in bed and i caress your head as gently and as violent as you like it. you tell me that it's your favourite feeling. day after day, i search for familiarity in you. sometimes i wonder if you have an existence. maybe you exist only as words in my head. you lie unmoved, and our life lies unchanged. i'm losing you.

being. i've been in love. back to when the holly touched the mistletoe, i touched you for the last time. our bodies danced across the day and our smiles remained frozen to our lips. i painted you on the rocks by the riverside, and oh how deeply you adored it. i remember looking up at the starlit sky and wishing that this moment would last forever, no matter how cold your hands were growing by the second. we lie under the Christmas tree as i open my eyes just to realise that i am dreaming. i glance back at the empty hallway i stand in. i sense familiarity. a whiff of your plum cake. i will miss sharing it with you.
yet once again i take your hand and spin you across the garden. if it's a sin to be with you then so be it. norms of this world fail to reach me when it comes to you.

there is a stranger sitting by the lake. there is a mighty stranger with kind eyes. she wraps herself in my arms and tells me that she might get lost today. i nod in sheer agreement and understanding. she motions towards my lips and scurries closer, asking for a glass of wine. neither of us are completely awake. she tells me that she might die today. i nod in sheer agreement and understanding. i am close behind her, intermittently warm, just so she could fall back upon me.

you're turning colder, colder as i hold you. you remind me of snow. of snow, snowballs and of joy. your eyes are a trip to everything that i hoped our life would contain. but now they're empty. maybe you don't exist other than the words in my head. your eyes don't remain anymore. i shut them with my fingertips. i close mine as well and try to remember you.

a voice whispers, "wine?"

you look so beautiful in death, my love. perhaps you've finally overcome your worldly grievances. i stroke your hair gently as i say goodbye to you. my body won't settle in the present, but yours has. and i want to fall in love with you in this moment, but that seems near to impossible. your skin has turned to the colour of your wedding dress. you look so content that i couldn't complain even if i desired to. yet i weep and i weep but you're nowhere close to waking up. this is the end of Eden as we know it. your wedding dress looks the same as the day you first wore it. i just wish to rip it off and wake you up to life. no lover's melancholy can be contained in this garden. i must walk down to earth. i must resign to the mundane. i'm living in a paradise lost.

i never realised how deeply i loved you
till i lost you.
and then i could tell no one about how i loved you
they'd stare at me as if i'd said something completely
deranged;
they'd drain out my love for you.

now i wish to just hold you-
even though i never used to.
i wish now that i could have you,
because no matter how bad you stink of my blood,
i will always love you.

slam my head into walls trying to figure out why
you still persist endlessly in me
oh, how i wish to be close
to you.
for no matter how you stink of my blood;
i will always love you,
and i will never know why i do.

did the world end? when you let go of my hand?
i do not know
i am still by the lake,
mourning your absence.
the birds haven't sung,
and the wind doesn't blow,
Eden's doors won't open.
i am still by the lake,
mourning you.
the flames outside my window
don't mean a thing
your loss is fuller,
it burns my insides
till i have no breath
left in me.
gasping for your love,
always knowing that it was never there.

we did not get you to a graveyard,
buried you right beside your palm tree.
we didn't level the soil
we just let you lie there
like you would every week,
on a casual Sunday morning.
you just lay there waiting,
for the earth to take you as its own.
we didn't spread any ashes
you just frolicked around
like you would,
on a casual Sunday morning.

oh no, we did not
throw away your bedsheets,
for you'd wake up anytime
to come sing your Sunday song;
shaking with mirth till your sides ache-
hugging me ever so tightly.

we did not take you to a graveyard
we buried you beside your palm tree,
and you laughed with us
just like a casual Sunday morning.

the world is moving, moving away from me. the world is moving on but i'm stuck right here, perhaps for the rest of my life. the world doesn't remember you, but i do. the world will let me down soon. the world will walk away while i'm still glued to the same spot. the dream that you're alive still haunts me. people are catching up with the pace of the present. i wonder why i am still here. maybe i am the weak link after all. what i have left of you now is only the rose in my hand. this rose reminds me of all our terrible times, and how every second of it was worthless. all that time spent arguing i could've spent with you, happy. life fazes me. the world has already walked away from my side. only *i* am what is left of *me*. the rose is wilting, petal by petal, and so is the memory of you. i am guilty. i am guilty of not framing you on my walls and of not cherishing you enough. i am guilty of not leaving you when you were with me, because now the memory of you refuses to leave my side.

and maybe i could stitch a beautiful tapestry out of your loss. but it would be all quiet and colourless. nothing beautiful remains anymore. nothing would succeed in replicating your madness. my surroundings are losing their colour. maybe the blank inside my headspace is absorbing it all. today, as i feel a stinging absence, i feel like parts of me may be painfully subsiding. nothing is as beautiful as it used to be. the air lies still. the world is mundane without you. a can of stale soup. i'm living in a paradise lost.

i feel unusually quiet,
like someone forbade me to talk-
i only stare about now,
let my words die like dominoes upon themselves.
sometimes i almost
open my mouth
to say something
but then realise that
i am probably
wrong,
or redundant.
what's the point anymore
i feel an unusual heat at the end of my throat
contrary to how it's a
cold graveyard of my sentences,
lingering quiet.
maybe i've lost the art of conversation?
or maybe my mind is too loud.
i'm not smart enough,
to know which.
i feel unusually quiet
like the loud corners of my mind
shut down their perpetual motion
at an abrupt instant
at a sudden decision

i feel no urge to compensate
no sound pleases me
i just want to leave

the day the guitar strings broke,
you told me a story-
of blue oceans and sails,
and of white prophecies.

the day the strings broke,
you told me that your mom was doing good
and your dad had left six years ago.

the day the strings broke,
fireflies sat on your nose
and you held my hand
and told me you were home.

the day the strings broke
you told me you were diagnosed with
late stage cancer
and the fireflies bled into darkness.

the day the strings broke,
you kissed my forehead
said you're leaving home
did you say goodbye?
we will never know

the day the strings broke,
your mother returned crying
i bought you your favourite flowers,
and laid them upon your cold throat.

the day the strings broke,
i realised that i was alone
and an emptiness was born in my stomach,
you were never coming home.

the day the strings broke,
i felt your absence
for now you'll never tell me stories
and i'll never give you hope.

the day the strings broke,
i wrote a song for you
and you held my hand;
and told me you were home.

for i have forgotten
what creativity feels like
i feel so much weight
all words have lost meaning

i love you,
i love the mole on the back of your head,
but you're gone.
no one tells me
if the wind still blows
my voice simply echoes through every
night and day.

i love you,
i love the mole on the back of your head,

yet everyday
i float through
oceans of gold
hoping i sail into you,
hoping i sail into a time
where i can see you,
and your memories are real.

like ascending levels in a video game, i continue my quest for you. i find my daughter's face in every corner of the world, lingering quietly in a sweet silence. i kiss her goodnight and i walk off the earth looking for you.
i belong in blank white rooms devoid of noise. i belong in white beaches by a garden. white canvases full of your face. empty white lilies perched on your grave. blank tapes documenting your loss. it's comical how you're always on my mind now. maybe you really begin to exist more the moment you are gone.

as i walk down this road of lilies, i figure i have nowhere
to go.
all the streets are white,
and the world is mourning you
my mind is white,
and so very full of you.
you sit by the lake, and you bring me flowers-
one by one you put them in my hair.
we share a glimpse
and you smile,
how do i ask for your name?

and i sit by the lake in pursuit of you-
day by day as the sun goes down,
we share a glimpse,
and you smile-
how do i forget your name?

i've spent most of my life
believing that i will find you in the sky
the sun holding your smile
like you always did.

i've spent most of my life
believing that you live in the sky
so much more fuller than before
for every time i've looked up,
i've seen you, always you,
trying to have a word with me
through another world.
to complete every sentence that you left unsaid.
and maybe i'll carry you in me forever
for the sake of this world.
i hope you carry me in yourself,
for the sake of yours.

you will never leave me,
i will never let you.

i will leave this world,
the day i leave you

i spend my nights under the sky
hoping you visit me through a star
and you flicker to make me smile,
so i know that you're here with me.

i will spend countless days writing about you
because all the notebooks you left me
they crave your touch,
your name,
and your eyes.
so now they speak about you,
night and day

they will never forget your name.

i will never be lonely now
because now i know that in your world,
you are always looking for me too.

reaching out through your sun
touching my leaves as gently as you could.

and if i spend most of my life
looking at the sky trying to find you-
i will never regret it,
because carrying you within myself
makes me the proudest of myself.

i always miss half of me
but when i look at the sky,
you look back at me
and i'm complete.

your memories
melt away to a staircase
"Nadia" my heart screams,
i come down to earth.

Chapter Two

spring

memento mori

and today i will fall in love with you, and today i will fall through the ocean. i don't know what it is in the rocks that intoxicates me. i will float my love letters for you in the water hoping they reach your world; be it Eden or earth. i will whisper your address to the waves, and i will laugh when they tell me they don't know where that is. i don't dream when i close my eyes anymore. i'm dreaming only with my eyes open now. i've been here for days. my feet are getting cold. perhaps i live on this rock now. i look at my letter, and i realise that i've casually run out of words. i weep and i weep on the paper hoping they emerge out as words. and i smudge a drop of wine on the paper, just so you know that it's me.

stupid paranoia
disgusts my spine
as i sit fumbling at my desk,
with the same rectangular white sheets,

my thoughts are reclining on
amphetamine, and mourn
all of the pages torn.
i will stop trying to remember you.
you do not exist.

sometimes i wonder how you are doing. and as soon as
that thought passes by me i delve right into it. maybe it
is not for me to care about.
maybe we're really over.

i want to ask you if the birds
still sing because,
ever since you lied to me
they've all been silent.

i pass by so many crowds
i wonder if you're in there,
have you ever looked at someone in a distant car
and wondered how their day was,
and what led them here?
maybe that is the best kind of love
strange, unknown.

and when the city
starts to look like stars
i wonder if i've left
my home behind
or if this feeling is now
home

every time i close my eyes
i travel to a new sky
a new sea,
pavements i haven't walked-
and people i haven't met.

he dreamt of travelling the world
but what are airplanes
when she's got thoughts
to colour the maps
and sail the rafts
in countries we
haven't heard of.

somehow my heart aches for you everyday. i am surprised that i still remember what you look like. my girl, my girl from another world. you were god's mismanagement of life and death. home is lost, and home is many seas away. you are lost, you are so many memories away. i think we realised the might of your reign after your reign was over. it's comical how humane this phrase is and yet none of us never seek to learn from it. day and night i am sinking into the sand. but i'll pick you up, one grain of sand at a time, and put you back together. my girl, my girl from another world. your tears continue to mould my days same as your laughter. i weep to the ocean about you often, hoping your memory floats away in tears. i'm never well equipped to heal from your loss, i need you in continuum. your absence will never go away. the ocean may gape wider, yet it never takes your place. you were truly wondrous. i feel it now that you are truly missing. i wish i could bury you in my heart.

beyond the fields of life and death,
i was there-
right on top of the world.
there was pure happiness surging through me
and in that moment i didn't care if i
lived or died,
if i stayed afloat or jumped right into the ocean,
because i was simply so alive
breathing in the salt and the drugs.
it wasn't a physical location
but wherever i was,
i was so purely happy.
i had spiritual contentment-
waves licking my feet,
offering me death,
i wanted to jump right in
and float away
to wherever the universe takes me.
i don't know if it was the drugs or the hormones,
but life flowed through me
blooming,
through every gush
how i wish that
every day is
just like
this.

by the stairway to heaven,
someone called to me,
and i rushed-
slipping on rocks,
living on the edge,
psychedelic delusions.

i thought of no one,
i belonged to no one,
and no one belonged to me.
i belonged to the universe, and the universe belonged to
me.

and i've never had a love,
fuller than myself.
lacking but making up
slowly mending
all the blue
and holding myself
tighter till i feel okay.

listening to this song makes my neck shiver. my senses tingle. it throws me back to a phase of life where you were so close and unknown.
but now that i can touch you, it suddenly loses all its significance. i have lost ability to convey the feeling. it's probably the feeling of absolute safety when you take me around the neighbourhood.
crowded rooms, empty words. just two guitars and a beer.

all of it feels simply unknown now. but life is throwing all of it back to me.
day by day, you crawl back to me. the beige essence of life is trickling back into my veins with the comfort of your laugh.

what a funny feeling this song gives me.
strange nostalgia, yet seemingly unknown. made up of memories we never made, spawning.
i've never known that i could be so full. but i am now. i am today. full of life as we knew it. the life we had lost, the life we will have.

all i remember is a smudge of you and everyone else. it's almost like a distant memory. falling into each other's souls, two guitars and a beer. never making any sense, not really.

i wish for my head to fall asleep soon. i wish to heal away from your long tantrums. heal away from being your muse. i am me now. simply me.

but this song will never cease to be perfect.
and this song will never cease to remind me of you.
time after time.

the world will elude us soon. but we will keep walking and we will keep falling into the ocean. in this world, you and i will reunite, and you and i will be lost and found a million more times. you walk on feathers in my bedroom, and you poke at my puppet-limp-carcass. inside my mind you're a funny, funny feeling. i'm not sure if i remember you the way that you wanted me to. a tunnel vision of us in the future fazes me. maybe love should cease the second it starts to get cold hearted. but again, maybe it's all a part of getting lost and found with each other. a distant radio blares the music to our first dance, and we've found each other again, and with your head on my chest, we're terribly smitten in a childish love, dancing away.

being. i've been in love. i've spent a nasty amount of time looking for my mind. i'm homesick for my homely liquid, but you kiss away my thoughts and take me by the hand. we walk over glass shards and you take me through your seven gates. we come to a garden so loud, so green and so full of people and their songs, that it spills my brain. my thoughts lie aloof and molten on the floor. and i collapse and there's no telling what this night is going to morph into. i collapse and perhaps i am allowed to. your skin resembles a calm, white moon. i collapse atop you and you never fail to love me, and you kneel down to my cathedral of bones. on earth, and in this garden, we have always been one. this garden might not be perfect, and in that lies my peace. i cry into your arms and i pray to god that i never fall in love. i close my eyes as the buzz fills my ears. my head aches from their pointless screeching. i cry out of pain. but you tell me that as long as i have sat around in their peace, i should be the one to sit around in their chaos as well.

and for every time i feel like i've lost you,
a butterfly flies past me-
and i follow you,
i follow you, through my mind.
you run about so carelessly,
in the mustard fields of memory,
your face glows a strange reminiscent yellow.
you're in your grand white dress
you look to me in search of something
and the tiresome shiver of familiarity climbs my spine.
and we circle back to our marriage day,
you hold out your hand to me-
is violence always a mistake?

i love you,
i love the mole on the back of your head,
but here i am
in the mustard field of memory
under a sky full of stars,
dying an absurd death without you.

i live in a seashell with my wife. i sleep on the cold floor. i dance along the calcareous edges of my home, and the paths keep curving. my feet are caked in mud, and they've been calling me an earthling. me and my wife, we run along the coastline hand in hand every morning. earth is beautiful in a way Eden could never be. earth can contain my melancholy in a way Eden won't i hope you find your place in life. i hope you find your home because i never will. i've gone too far in life worshiping lords who aren't mine, so far so that i don't think i retain a sense of home and of belonging anymore. i got lost in too many places that weren't home to begin with. i fell too in love with the place farthest from home. life has struck me with too many women to call my mother. i don't belong in a home. i am a child of the ocean. time after time i fall into the ocean, because the ocean does not want to name me. the ocean doesn't deem me the creator of the universe. the ocean deems me endless. in the ocean i remain purely myself. in the ocean i am just its drops of water. i am not required to be great. it sets me free like your love used to. with the ocean i am nowhere and everywhere, all at once.

life was anarchy
when i knew you loved me.
your hands danced over the piano-
and glued stars to the sky.
life was anarchy,
when life was perfect.
and with no strife to fret upon,
creativity had lost its sense.

july, a bird croaked
and life was blessed with death
maybe utopia exists,
but utopia never lasts
my heart cries for you!
but then i wake up.
memento, memento mori.

Chapter Three

summer

amor vincit omnia

Nadia looks to me just like she used to on earth. time didn't lay out its puzzles in the ways we'd suspect. time ran you up and down my bad days, and time wove us in its clever play. from the midst of my mustard fields of memory you step out into reality, and you are simply unreal. you symbolise all the beauty this earth can contain, all of beauty there is. i will not attempt to put you into meagre words, as there is something so inexplicably divine about your eyes, stinging blue. we face each other, standing naked. my quest for you is finally over. but as i open my mouth to greet you, i realise that there is nothing i want to say to you. you smell like lilies. your skin glows a radiant yellow, and the colour shakes me awake. maybe i've touched you in another life.

where have i seen her before?

my sweet Nadia?

in a stupid dream, perhaps, is it?

and suddenly,
we were just voices talking under a lightbulb sun.
and how amazing it was-
to not really look at each other,
but into each other's thoughts.
swimming in and out
of our overlapping conscience.

as and when the moonlight receded, i couldn't feel you
as a separate being anymore. you felt true to me.
you felt close to me.
you felt like the nostalgic pinch of a lunch box lost
several years ago.
i had missed you terribly.

it was funny, and yet so beautiful how we spoke like
nothing had ever gone wrong with you and me.
years after years have gone by now,
i think the gaping hole has finally bridged over.
the past holograms smile to us like a distant memory.

we were just voices talking under a lightbulb sun,
laughing till our sides hurt, not caring who we woke up
in our mirth.
we didn't care much about the world.
but that was okay, because the world hadn't cared much
about us lately.
we were simply
children barefoot
running along every old lane,
expecting it to narrate bedtime stories
so we could finally
rest our bones.

you were such a
newfound purity
in a meaningless old conversation,
love reborn
on a slow Friday midnight.
new light
dawning upon us,
casting us into the trance
we waited for so long.
never really looking at each other
but knowing each other's soul.
completely.

-prelude to a kiss

your arms drown me in a familiar sense of comfort, though i've never been in them before. your soul kisses mine as we touch, and new love is born on a friday night. ever so flowing in and onwards into an ocean so red, the red tide draws me in and i grab your gentle hands, ever so soft and mesmerising. you grab my waist as we share a cigarette. i can feel waking up to you every morning. oh, how peaceful. i could only think of how deeply i desired you as i took your hand and spun you around. you radiate a homely peace, the type that quietens every second thought inside me and convinces me that i have found home. i was looking for you all along, in every failed lover. i sit opposite to you on a boat. i wish to sit here forever and float away to purgatory. i want to light the boat on fire and swim to a new country and make it our home. it's strange because i do not love you. i do not know what i feel. i feel a strange elation when i'm with you. i feel like every part of my body is at rest and in constant happiness and i will never be happier than when I'm with you. with you i am whole. every bit of me is satisfied in your smile. i stand with you hand in hand, and we simply remain. we don't kiss or talk or hug. we just remain, floating, not falling in or out of love, but smiling into each other's eyes, being each other's numbing pain. maybe you are my psychotic drug. this is the first day of my life. i wake up in a drugged high. with you i am the birds of the sky, flying away. with you, i'm endless. i could be anyone. you wake me up to life. you wake me up to what life could be. and maybe i know that we aren't meant to be. i know that we'd choose other people in the blink of an eye. but at the end of the day, you remain my wish, you remain my muse. my wish is to love you, and till the end, you are the first day of my life.

behind my eyes
in the headspace
you'll find countries which never existed.
i sit at your side, you tell me my eyes are blue
that they draw you in so deep
and make red kites fly across your violet skies
how does it matter that i will never see
any of this,
i can feel every word,
of every song you wrote
i sit by you, you tell me my face turns red,

did you paint the sky blue?
like i had asked you to?
or have you invented a pastel pink to surprise me?

can i afford
to fall another time?
maybe because i have already tripped over.

floating in the ecstasy
of an unknown love,
and unborn troubles
simply smitten.

i'm reaching out for you-
but
should i afford to fall another time?

maybe only if
you hold onto my hand,
and fall with me.

waste bags
full of memories
waste bags
full of our dates and dilemmas

and every time i try to throw them away,
you plant it right outside my door.

Nadia wakes me up to tell me that the pain is gone. and i spin her around in a vivid glory yet again. the paradise that we had lost is running right back to us. there are no longer walls between us and maybe it's funny that we smile all day. or is it torturous? i wake up by your side, but you run away by sunset. nothing feels right in this city, but at least i'm with you again.

i wonder what this numbness we feel is. i wonder if it is
love.
you ask me what the point is.
there is no point.
the point is being a parasite inside each other's hearts till
the numbness refuses to leave.

anything is an excuse to be with you
be it numbness, be it love.

funny how i water something
as indecisive as our love.
spiralling into it but,
never quite falling.
catching feelings but
hanging by a thread

your inhibitions,
my nerves.

i wonder what i look like in your life. i'm a thin sheet of ice when i'm with you. you touch my skin and my shards break away, my worldly self melts away. my silence overwhelms me. all my inhibitions fall to the ground, and i am in awe of what you are capable of doing to me.

wait for me,
for i have the world to explore-
but once i am done,
i promise that i
will come running right back to you.

i think you came to me as a realisation that i am human too.

you reminded me of the simplest things in life. you swim up from the lake and your head is adorned with a garland of lilies. lilies send a chill down my spine, but i think i've forgotten why. i think you came to me as a reflection of a strained past. my heart is buried in your thoughts. it's a shame that we'll never walk together again.

we stare into each other endlessly,
not being able to look away.
sometimes i wonder if we are falling,
knowing we aren't-
holding on to each other, scared, keeping you from
tumbling into all of it.

maybe the best kind of falling is floating
whispering sweet nothings,
no promises,
simply floating.

sometimes i wonder if we are meant to be. but the
answer is, that it does not matter.
as long as we are intertwined, mangled in each other's
string of truth and lies, you are mine and i am yours.

i remember watching you smile for the first time,
i must have been staring too hard
because i remember every single detail
and i remember it so well
i could paint you in a thousand words.

you, my love
are the face of everlasting beauty
you render all senses numb.
your face bears no angles
no conventional thoughts
no sociological imagination
no horrifying bluff
yet
i will never know you,
until i've known myself.
your beauty is introspection
your beauty is a curse
i will never know you
until i've known myself
you, my everlasting hearth.

i'm a prisoner of devotion. devotion has reduced me to grains of sand. i am no longer whole. i am no longer myself. it's so beautiful to forget life and run about what isn't and what *could* be. man speaks of vices and virtues, yet existence itself continues to be his self-slaughter.

with every goodbye, i felt my devotion dying. and now, i am a free bird. but i am merely a fragment of my full self. i no longer remain a person you would approach.
existence is nothing but a fleeting dream without her. i am going nowhere without my sweet Nadia. no hills are as gentle without her, no song as sweet.

blue.
her hair tinged with hints of blue.
blue
the home she's always longed for,
she found in the ocean.
if i lost all my colours,
and all my thoughts,
would you remind me what love felt like?
or would you get drunk
on my ignorance.
but oh, would you be so kind
and colour me blue
so for once i could be
home.

i wish i could capture those moments with you,
and turn them into pictures.
just those little moments
when you laugh;
shaking with mirth.
i wish i could capture those moments
when you look at me
with eyes filled with a distant charm.

i wish i could capture those little moments when we both
smile;
and how i wished those moments would last
but you once told me
"everything that comes *together,*
eventually falls *apart.*"

oh summer, our passion is crumbling
i won't bask in your love,
it's not beautiful anymore.
hey summer
come back to me
i want to dance without you,
but without you, i'm crumbling.

oh summer, i wake up to your song
you bring back my dying breath
and kiss me alive
and like sleeping beauty i lie,
terribly happy, just to have you.
oh, summer.

your starving eyes linger on my skin day after day. i wonder what draws you to me, i can never tell. the size of our desires is unsettling. i wish we lived in two different worlds and never knew each other. you live in places of my heart i did not know exist. the size of our desires keeps me awake. your hungry fingers crawl closer to my skin. i want escape from our delicate love-prison. i think that maybe the hardest thing in life is balance, or maybe it does not exist in reality. gone are the days when i'd want to be stuck to you like a pair of smitten kids, because today, all your face does is haunt me. i don't think i'll ever be able to walk away from your life even if i wanted to. your eyes had chosen me with a firm satisfaction, and i had promised to never let go. but now that i've looked you in the eye for hours on end, i realise that you're the thing i hate the most in this world, and i'd do anything to rid myself of you. you render me non-existent. you trap me within myself. on some days, i feel like we are one person. i am nothing without you. your presence sucks out everything good about me. you make me irrelevant.

without you, i starve for completion. and i promise to myself that i will never let you be the one to complete me. but running you come, and i eat right out of your hand.

our memories are sitting by my side.
laughing at me,
our memories sting at my sides
they're cutting up my heart,
love flows within me as you walk out of my life
in vino veritas.

and maybe this is the end,
of life as we knew it
maybe this the end,
of everything we ever built.
we never knew
that such a twin flame could go its own ways
and we never knew
that we'd ever flow this way.

maybe we were never meant to-
live in a pretty house
with pretty flowers,
because maybe our *love* was never
enough for it.

a chance rendezvous of two strangers,
what a chance separation too.
maybe all of this was just a ruse
for me to start appreciating
everything i never did.

maybe you and i,
were a childish tale.
maybe we were never meant to meet,
and that's okay.

your train leaves 4 pm
scheduled megalomania.
you don't know if you want to run to it,
or let it crawl to you.
do you see the passengers?
do they look strange?
they're screeching on the red pavement of incomplete
goodbyes-
all stranded in the land of pale longings,
you lunge onto my arm hoping you fall asleep,
no minute has been longer, thoughts prolonging.
it's 3:59.
your train leaves at 4
you have one hand intertwined in mine
and another on the floor.

Chapter Four

fall

memento vivere

Aitijhya Mondal

Nadia has left flowers behind for me to find her, i'm
sure. petal after petal, i drift through continents hoping
to see her face. this dream keeps running out of my
control, but i'm willing to stay till the end of it because
of how terribly it fascinates me. i follow each rose in the
back of my mind carefully. and suddenly i'm
by the lake and
there's
Nadia with her lilies
swimming in a pool of
my blood.

and i'm running into your sweet arms of destruction
time after time,
just to feel
the comfort of a past life.

perhaps i've lingered in the thought of you for longer than i should. i live inside my thoughts, and with time i've come to realise as to how empty of a feeling desire is. desire loses all its being without what's being desired. a single loss, and your brain turns to stone and you become a mere vegetable of life. your hands move around in a perpetual motion, your legs function like they used to, but your mind has shut down. it has shut down beyond your control. you can only hear your bones move under the pressure of having to, all purpose is lost.

ask you why you hate your birthday,
even though i know the answer.
and watch tears bead up your eyes.

i don't remember you,
my last recollection of myself
is from nine months ago
the rest has smudged onto itself.
blurring lines between days,
and people.

and you
seem so far away
it's almost unreal how
i can almost touch you,
but i don't.

i visit my lover in dreams. in quiet whispers she comes to me. and just for a day, every bit of blue goes away. i sleep, and i sleep till i cannot remember what life feels like. minuscule letters from a newspaper pop up in the back of my head. cigarette smoke from months ago burns my skin. pictures of you hang limp on the wall. fear clenches my insides, and i touch my face and realise that it doesn't belong to me anymore. fear has taken over my face and body. what i continue to be to this world is simply a white mask, a childish mould. on some days i wish for my body to dissociate into sand particles and line up the ocean. you are the ocean, so very blue in my memories. it would finally make me whole with you.

once again you come to me in arpeggios.
you're my sepia among the rainbows.

in strange ways you always come back to me
and i never oppose it,
i let it flow.
because once i oppose it,
you'll be stuck in me forever.
but all i want is
you to completely flow out of me.
one day at a time,
memory by memory.

in strange ways she comes back to me
but i smile more than i frown,
because what is love without her
no ends, and no beginnings.

strings cut to make the ends meet
left you happy,
left me stranded,
but with time it appears
that i might be the one who was blessed.

i can feel five other renditions of me frolicking around in my mind. they circle around, ridiculing my skin. they're holding hands, telling stories, dancing through their hysteria, hoping to penetrate my skin and become i, me, mine someday. the anatomy of dependence has enslaved me. am i no longer contained within myself? my skin is failing to live through the day. my mind is crumbling, and as time stops, i can see you right in front of me. a cold sweat breaks out on my forehead and i go frantic in pursuit of you. i run for hours on end and stretch my arms out in desperation. i run and i run, but at the end of the day, i fail to touch you.

i still love her, in strange ways. not the kind of love that makes you long for someone and want to fall deep into their arms at the end of the day, but the kind of love you think back on and you feel complete. you smile, and feel this chill down your spine. because it was simply so beautiful how you gave yourself to someone, completely with no lines within yourself, no boundaries. it's almost unreal it ended. but that doesn't change how beautiful it was. how beautifully it changed me. i now know how *giving* is the most liberating thing that i will ever do. it's empowering.

i still love her like the wind still blows, and i probably always will.

you remember your first love, in a good way or bad. you remember because they show you every part of how the rest of your life will be. you remember because they showed you yourself, and everything you will be.

i pride myself in being able to open myself to the world. i pride myself because i was good to her. it's a shame it ended, but i am certain that it is for the best.

i'll love her, maybe forever. i'll love her for all the wrong she did to me. for every day how she made my insides feel like an unending spiral.

but maybe none of this will ever matter to you or to us. at the end of the day, you will forever be my first love and i will be yours.

i'm at crossroads with myself.
i'm at crossroads with what i want and what i need.
standing up with wind in my air,
singing out loud with your ghost.
what blue waters,
quite a dusty road,
i know that i'm going somewhere really great with you.
and we both know that we love the car, the journey, the
wind, and the view.
but some spirit in me keeps telling me to drive home.

and the mountains look so great,
and everyone else has booked their stay.
what a view,
and what a life,
but to me it seems that i
am running out of breath
every time i lunge at the peak.

still the mountains look so great,
sell every ounce of me to buy my breath
but maybe i'm not a trend setter
maybe i like the valley better.

have the mountains looked so great?
you look to me to find your way
your paths and maps are in my head
but it seems my legs have given way

will the mountains ever look so great
sell every ounce of me to buy my breath
but maybe i'm not a trend setter
maybe we like the valley better.

and if i
knew to be perfect
i wouldn't stare every time you blinked.

your weights
are so heavy
they bear me down.
some days i wish
you were
strong enough
to carry mine.
but,
your weights
are so heavy
i forget about mine
every day
ashamed
to even let out.
i am nothing,
but a mere listener.
you stab me,
you stab me,
you stab me,
and then complain about
how the knife was too heavy-
dusty-
old-
day after night,
i listen to my murderer
rant about how the blood on her hands,
looks ugly,
as i lie
motionless on the floor.

you bring out
whatever that's violent in me.

the quiet whispers of my father,
the cold touch of his knife.

when i stand talking to you
i watch myself from a distance
to see how my hands move like my father's
how my eyes burn with his quiet rage,
ignoring your every emotion
wanting your blood to trickle down
my wrists.

you bring out my violence
bright and red
blooming like the
iridescence of our garden,
where the flowers never grew.

my heart longs for you hurt
because in how you've left me
ruined.
i've tried to forgive you,
but my heart couldn't surrender

and in forgiving you
time after time,
i've wanted your blood on my hands.
trickling down
and watering our garden,
hoping the flowers finally bloom.

and today i've stopped coming up for air
i've decided to sit right here for years
and bask in the warmth of the ocean.

and none of your goodwill will ever reach me. no one will ever touch me. but you do. you shake me awake, and you watch all my layers come off. your eyes linger on my skin, they're never apart. and you bite into my skin, blood in your mouth. my arms won't move. neither will my body. you bite away chunks of me and sing me a lullaby. i fall asleep. none of your goodwill will ever reach me.

and why would i want to look back
if looking away
healed my soul.

i stand in a labyrinth of burning people. burning family. no one looks me in the eye, all of their faces are buried in shame. my question remains that maybe if i deserved the fire too. or have i been kind enough to the world? i watch my best friends struggle to breathe as they lunge at my feet. a lunge for life. a lunge for redemption. but i have nowhere to go. no reason to forgive. my circle of kindness is final and complete.

what does it take to forgive? i chase you down lanes of grey. yet you don't forfeit. maybe human emotions are supposed to be a very clever puzzle. none of you found your way out, all of you stand burning in an inhumane overdose of feelings. and i stand here, void of emotions, watching my family burn to the ground. should it be sad that i'm the only one left behind? but maybe a solitary life isn't so bad after all. i am not able to shut my eyes, so i gape in awe at the tiny elegance of death.

death, what a small price to pay for love.

i wish i knew who you were before i kissed you.
i never knew you.
you were the sepia flowing through my veins,
plain and uninteresting.
never standing out,
blending in the background,
bleeding through my walls.
your unfamiliarity quietens me
and i forget who i am.
i wish i knew who you were
before i looked you in the eye and told you that
i loved you.

i remember a green trance.
being. i've been in love.

trance filled my ears as the world around me started
fading away, crumbling completely to a holographic
fever dream.
you kept calling out for me, but i was dead in a green
trance, convulsing.

and every time i opened my eyes,
i saw god.
wondrous
and strange
and yet
you were so out of my reach.

i remember you yanking my motionless arm and
smacking my head on the wall out of love. *how pure.*
the ill effects of alcohol will never fail to amaze me, but
funny thing is there was none. i'll never know what was.

you were a sepia shadow melting through my euphoric
stance. you were a blunt ghost any day of the year. veins
would never appreciate you.
i reach, and i reached for you, but it was all loss. my
hands were on the table, and you were out the door. i lay
there. waiting. waiting to be saved. someone's wine
glass on the table. waiting. waiting to be devoured.

but you were a fool, and i was a nomad. me waiting for
you would be your biggest delusion. i was not the one to
wait even a mere moment. none of you or them mattered
to me. i was my own, mine, me muse.
but the blood. the blood trickling down the sides of your
wrist. i think about it every day. i wish those scars never
heal for you. i'd be grateful.
but there's no fear. and there will never be. it's all pure
holographic fun. no blood intended. but even if there is, i
know that my rocks will remain. the rocks will drown
me out and save me time after time, engulfing me in a
sober maze i cannot and wouldn't try to escape. the
rocks are evermore euphoric than your substance. they
pull me back to surface and anchor me and my faith.
maybe after every sentence, the *rocks* are my muse. i am
but a mere nobody.
some days i wish i fell into the ocean. and what a lovely
way it would be, to get carried away and let your faith
flow. especially that evening, it's funny how much i've
glorified it in my life, though a lot of it, once again, is a
white desire. dripping of violence.
but i am going nowhere, i'm stuck to my rocks. i love
being here. in this sense, i'm everything but a nomad.
but the facts that the rocks do exist, make me everything
i've ever wanted to be.
i'll be wandering till my feet let me.

when life lacked sunlight,
i sacrificed my dreams to get it back.
but now that my life is full
and all the windows are big – i've
decided that i never really liked
any of it.

and every fall,
your lullaby will fail to put me to sleep.
do you think it was
the minor key that kept me awake-

would you get mad if i chose to
silently close the door behind me?
as the words escape my mouth
i fail to stutter, you fail to look me in the eye.

dew lined up our pupils
and pierced the stone-cold veil
intertwined, you make me promise-

"if i ever wanted to leave,
i'd bid you a proper goodbye
with one day full of life."

cotton candy,
then stars.

as i turned away from you
and prepared not to look back,
what a heavenly sight
what a heavenly sigh

i'm here.
and i'm distant.
i stand between white walls,
torn between every colour that i
could choose to
represent myself.

i wake up in all probability.

the white is drowning me out. the uncertainty of you
stings at every corner of my body. i am streaming away,
never perfectly aiming.
i am simply floating along the continents, really. head as
empty as the ocean. i need a break. but i can't swim.

in between quiet seconds
i'll think about you.

i promise you,
i always do.
in between quiet seconds
i think about you-
and my mind repulses;
and grabs you by the collar
to throw you down the cliff.

the essence of being lost in an unknown city is unreal. there's comfort in being lost. my body and mind are liquid, my body and mind are now the air of this city. it's lovely and pure to die now, because there's no one that can help me. and i do not run about endlessly because in this city, i know that i am purely alone, and its inhabitants strange. so i just close my eyes in a careless sleep and hope never to be found. help is already way beyond me. i don't carry ownership of my life anymore. i belong to the people of the city now. maybe everyone i meet now is my family, yet somehow i manage not to know their last names.

but there's no clause to fret upon. they embrace my decaying corpse and pick me up and dust me. they take me to their little homes, and sit me down with a meal, and somehow in a matter of seconds i am a part of their week and day, suddenly family. i keep on living, in endless joy and laughter with strangers who know my second name but speak a different language than i do, seemingly complete. with every passing day, their voices begin to sound like comfort. but the city loses colour the second it starts to get familiar to me. maybe it is one of the same loops of life, just in a different city.

and when life starts to get black and white again i pack up my bags without a second thought. it remains the only sensible thing to do. i join my hands in peace and thank my friends for the life that they've given me.

and then i run. and i never look back. being taken care of and given a new life in a time of loss is a boon. but if i am no longer bound to loss, why would i want to be bound to a city? i run till the surroundings elude me. i have no sense of where i am anymore. i am lost yet again, but this time there's a strange comfort in being lost. i lie and roll about in mud, praising the rainbows behind my eyes. all of life lives inside of me. i am life. i am thriving.
the earth is receding
and my body is all green; i see your outline.
you disappear into Eden
and howling, i crawl by your side.

i returned to Eden and i searched for the moon, but
it was way beyond my reach. i've left it behind on earth.
far along the distance the only two moons i can see are
your eyes, the only moons i can ever have. in a world of
torment and bloody moons, i can finally see us having a
good life. i hold you under the stars and you whisper to
me,
"you're all the red that the moon can contain. in a world
of torment and bloody moons, you belong to *me*."

when i look at you, i feel my garden race back to me through your eyes. no matter where we might be, you always remind me of my hometown, and it's almost unreal how. your eyes spiral into the streetlights of my lost neighbourhood. i linger around the garden, the white in your eyes show me the empty caverns, your pupils are wet from the November rain. i want to bathe in the wet earth and hug the grass. i remember being comically tired of the people around me, but it's funny that the only thing i crave now is their presence and their touch. i wish that all the friends i've lost along the way would rise out of the mud and laugh with me. the air tastes like sweet love, and i feel a nudge on my shoulder. i turn around to see the only pair of eyes i recognise. my mother's eyes. i feel warm, the chemicals are spreading all through my body. my mother's image is getting clearer, and so is the desire to fall right into her arms. her eyes numb the prolonged wounds of time. even with the greatest of solitudes embracing me, she was right here. my preliminary concepts of comfort, reimagined. i am naked, and my memory is well forgotten. we are naked, and we are by the lake yet again. my corpse lies cold, waiting for the earth to take it as its own. you lie giggling besides me as if i've told the world's greatest joke. you take my hand, and i'm turning colder, colder as you hold me. and when we come back to life, you and i may not be whole, but our souls are always going to remain home.

Epilogue

every day i wake up,
and i dream of you.
"dream a little dream of me tonight",
you said.
and as we walked towards purgatory hand in hand,
i'm blindfolded and never questioning a thing you say.
is *love* what it takes to forgive the greatest of sins?
today as i close my eyes in the name of love
i just wish to open them again.

through the walls of purgatory,
you come to me in ripples-
and i wake up,
just to find that i am dreaming
and my eyes won't open
they're glued shut
i'm painlessly blind.
i'm asleep.

paracosm

/ˈpæɹəˌkɒz(ə)m/

noun

a detailed imaginary world created purely inside
someone's mind, this world may involve humans,
animals and things which don't exist in reality; or it may
also contain entities that are completely otherworldly.

hallucination

/həˌluːsɪˈneɪʃ(ə)n/

noun

an experience involving the apparent perception of something not present.

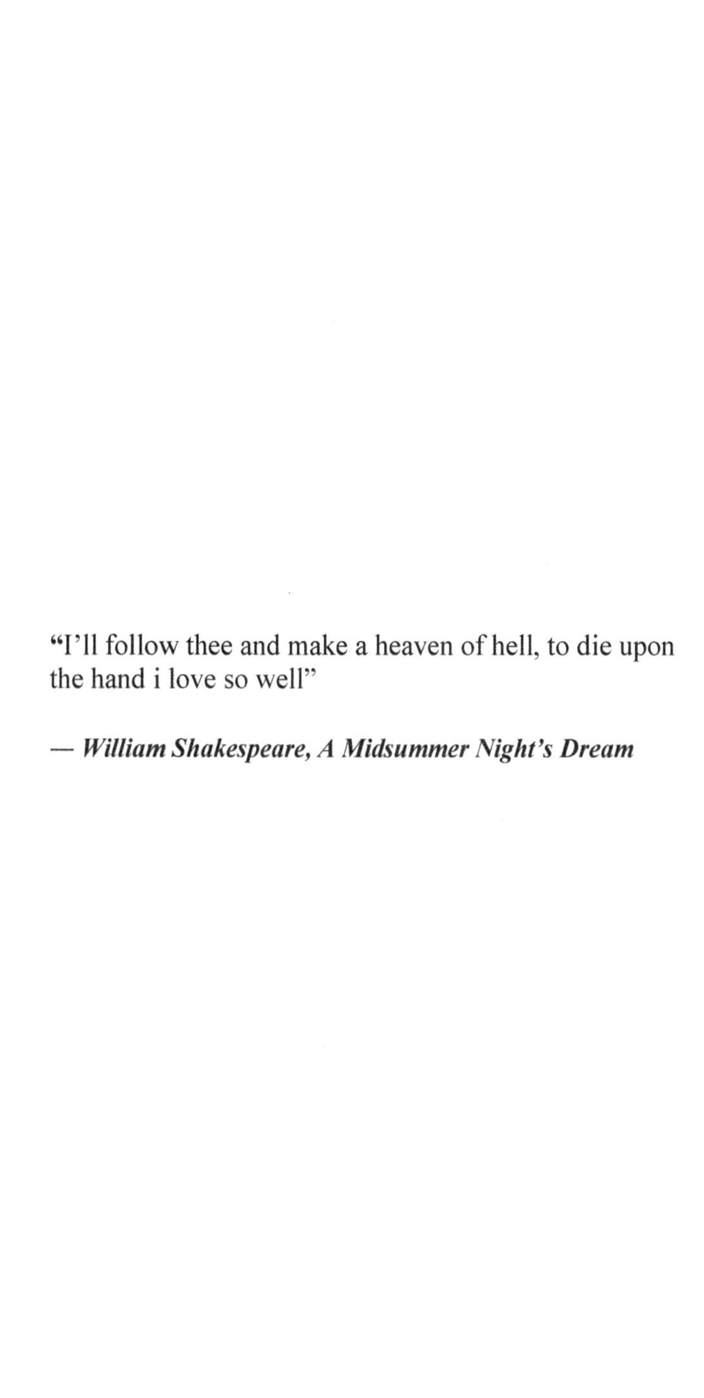

"I'll follow thee and make a heaven of hell, to die upon the hand i love so well"

— *William Shakespeare, A Midsummer Night's Dream*

ABOUT THE AUTHOR

aitijhya mondal is a 16 year old author and poet from kolkata, india. having started at a very young age, the budding literary figure has already co-authored seven anthologies with different publishing houses. she gained popularity primarily through her social media account which she often adorns with her beautiful poetry. you can visit her on instagram at @tizzysphotos. she endeavours to embark upon poetry as a career in the future.

Writer's Pocket

Writer's Pocket is a publication house established in 2016. We began with the aim of providing a better publishing platform for aspiring writers and budding poets.

The publishing industry in India (and around the world, to a great extent) is always something of a mystery even to the writers themselves. We are working on making publishing more accessible to everyone.

So far, we have helped over 3,000 writers turn their dreams into reality by publishing the books and continue to do so. By doing so, we also provide some of the best content by Indian writers to the readers.

Want to read more books? Scan this QR code with your smartphone and check out all our books on Amazon.